MW00780022

Also by Edward Alderette

An Alzheimer's Journey: Carolyn's Return to Birth

Other Volumes in the Wakefulness Series:

*Meditations, Contemplations and Reflections
About Awareness*

Sutras: Intentions to One's Higher Power

Qualities of Searchers

Volume 2 of the Wakefulness Series

Edward Alderette

ISBN: 978-0-9997989-2-8

1. Spiritual life-Meditations. 2. Poetry. 3. Awareness. 4. Reflection.
5. Cognitive behaviorism. 6. Philosophy. I. Title

DEDICATION

I dedicate these meditations, contemplations and reflections about qualities to those looking for an oasis when life feels like a desert.

ACKNOWLEDGMENTS

I thank my friend Cathy Carignan and niece Eileen Knott for their help with the transcription, formatting and publication of my writing.

CONTENTS

INTRODUCTION

This is a series of stories about specific qualities written over the course of a two-year period. In most instances, in this collection I have grouped three qualities together and I tell a story about a "him" or a "her" in relation to that trilogy. One trilogy for instance is Love, Respect and Appreciation.

It can be said of qualities — as of many other things — that they are at once the essence of simplicity and simultaneously as complex as a profound conceptual framework.

These stories address the duality of human qualities.

There is no hidden meaning in how the qualities are grouped together, but had they been grouped differently, the resulting story about them would have been totally something else.

Edward Alderette

IN THE PRESENCE OF THEIR PRESENCE

She inquired after vortices
Of energy
Which have the power
To connect
One to the flowing energies
Of the universal flow
Of things
And events
And ideas
And peoples
To "all that is."

She delighted in placing
Her presence in their presence
And enjoyed
The resulting bliss
Of the two coming together
Even if only
For an instant of an instant
As those things are known
To occur.
She returned to those vortices
And humbly waited
For their magic to simply be.

PATTERNS OF THE UNIVERSE

She sought
And meandered
In the forests
Where she knew
Wise trees to exist
And she followed the paths
Outlined by their wisdom
Even when
She was not sure
She understood...
She accepted
And gave those paths
A chance to reveal
And when revelation
Did come
She acknowledged
And contemplated
The gems
And even grains of golden dust
Of the patterns
Which make up
The universe...

BEAUTY

She had learned
almost intuitively
How to appreciate
What was beautiful
And knew to remain focused
On the beautiful
For it to continue
The lending of its energy.

She strove
To be one who evoked
Beauty
From the un-carved rock
And grew
In the awareness
That it was
The un-carved block
Within her
Which unfolded
As she engaged in creativity.

SHREWDNESS, INSIGHT AND AWARENESS

Unwittingly, he found himself
Intensifying his role as a
Seeker every time he felt
The urge to ask the powers
Of the universe to bestow
Upon him and those he loves
Energy in the form of
Perspicacity and
Insight and
Awareness.
In seeking perspicacity, he
Meant to grow in the ability
To grasp the lessons which
Life's patterns and events
Teach to those attentive
To expanding their comprehension
Of the bits and pieces
Of "what is."
Seeking insight reflected
His wanting to want
To be intuiting with
That aspect of intelligence
Which "knows"
Through a higher energy-level
Than what comes
With the power of logic.

While requesting life (energy)
In the form of awareness,
He simply sought to grow
In going to that level
Of consciousness which
Experiences the frequency
At which being vibrates,
At which being itself vibrates.

KINDNESS, GENEROSITY AND COMPASSION

He surmised that it had
To have been sheer
Inspiration of the first
Caliber the day on which
It occurred to him to
Formally ask for life
In the form of energy
In the form of
Kindness and
Generosity and
Compassion,
And it was of life itself
That he made this request
For it is from life that
All flows.

In the very act of asking
There was the sense
Of experiencing
What kindness had felt like
When he had encountered
It in real life and
In seeking to have
Generosity
In order to be able to have
More generosity to distribute
He seemed to access what

It felt like when it
Had been freely distributed to him.

He continued discovering
That the more he asked
For life in the form
Of compassion, the more
He grew in understanding
What he was asking for.

This alone prompted him
Even more to want
For himself and for those he
Loved, life in these forms
Of: Kindness and
Generosity and
Compassion.

BEAUTY, HARMONY AND SIMPLICITY

...not even aware that she
Was entering the station of life
Of the aesthetic one she would
Often request of the entire
Universe,
Life (energy) in the form of
Beauty
And harmony
And simplicity.

In that same role
She expressed heartfelt
Gratitude for
The beautiful and
The harmonious
Which had already
Graciously graced her life
And she was able
To flow into accessing
The moment of oneness
Which the experience of simplicity
Had already visited
Upon her in her artistic
Activity.

And it came to pass and
Kept on passing that the more

The universe responded
To her request, the more
The artist soul grew
And so too,
Grew the desire
To seek the beautiful
Fully in abundance to those
Who know how to observe
And there also flourished
Keen appreciation for
The ever present harmony
Amidst the daily cacophony
And there grew too
The ability to sense
The utter simplicity of the wavelength to which
All the material can be
Reduced,
Thus able, for instance, "to see"
The snowflakes it took
To give form to that glacier
The size of Patagonia.

SPIRALS OF FIERY RIBBONS

He would put himself away
As far as he could
From the galaxy:
The Milky Way.
At times, he would go away
As far as Andromeda
— guesstimated to be
At most 1,500,000 light years
From where he stood.
And from there
He would peer
At the spinning spiral:
The Milky Way.

With magnification devices
He would zoom into the center
Of where all that entire
Milky Way is spiraling into:
The place called:
Its black hole,
Which far from looking
'black'
Appears more akin to
Spirals upon spirals
Of fiery ribbons
Of billions of blazing suns
Swirling round and

Around to the vortex
Not seen to his eyes
Even with magnifiers.

He would assay
To spot and hold-in-focus
That one solar system
To which his earth
Is but a planet
And he would do so
Just to be aware
Where in all that
Dynamic flow
That solar system is
In that its native galaxy
Before it begins
To disappear into that giant eddy —
From which not even
Light can escape-
As it surely will be
Disappearing
Some day
Before
The sun starts to set
Forever.

HEALTH, WEALTH AND HUMOR

He accustomed himself
To ask — with total confidence —
The powers of the universe
For health in the same
Breath that he requested
Wealth and humor.

The latter, he liked to point
Out, we need, especially,
When the former two are
In shorter supply than we
Normally want.

The humor he sought was
The ability to be sensitive and
Alert to that recondite aspect
Of human nature which
Knows how to evoke
Risibility within the human
Soul even if only by bringing
A smile to the inner self
Or the slightest of mirth
To that human spirit.

The wealth he aspired to
Was, first and foremost,
To honor the dictum of the

Tao Te Ching
To know how to look for
And to find
"Fortune in misfortune"
And the health he wanted
To want was energy
In the form of growth
For his mind, body and spirit.

There was never a time
When he asked for life
In these three forms
That he didn't also request
As much for all those
People in his litany of
The ones he had loved in
His lifetime.

LOVE, RESPECT AND APPRECIATION

One day when he was feeling
A particularly stinging
Reversal of good fortune,
He remembered
That the universe —
Which he and all reality
Participate in —
Happens to be
A treasure trove of a
Cornucopia of an infinite
Set of possibilities
And so it dawned on him
To formulate the request
For love
Respect and
Appreciation.

As if, by inspiration —
For he knew not how to methodically plan
Such an act —
He began feeling
That if only he had
Three seeds
He could husband them
With all his might
So that they could grow
To something mightier

Than whatever he had
Heretofore imagined.

The seeds he found himself
Requesting of the powers
Of the universe were
The seeds of
Love
Respect and
Appreciation.

He was vowing
While he was asking
That, with life in these
Forms of energy,
He would engage immediately
In the cultivation
Of him being one of
The manifestations
Of life's love
Life's
Respect and life's
Appreciation.

He interpreted
The fulfillment of being
Which he was – there
And then – experiencing
As the gestation and
The growing of those
Three distinct
Seeds of life, then and there.

Ever since, whenever
He engages in the
Attention to these
Three life forms and
Manifestations,
He grows in the realization
That just as
The universe sees itself

Through our eyes
(As that one seer points out to us)
And experiences the awareness of its existence
Through our awareness,
So too, life manifests
Love,
Respect and
Appreciation through our
Cultivation of these
Very realities.

AS FORTUNE WOULD HAVE IT

As fortune would have it
A perception awakened
In her consciousness
One day
That to find paths of meaning —
Fullness in this existence
One does well
To explore experiencing
The reality of quietness
The reality of stillness
And
The reality of the oneness
Of the former two, synergistically
Combined.

As fortune would have it
It was because on that day
She happened to be
In the quietness of her inner space
And in the stillness
Of her motionless body
And in the oneness
Of that simultaneous
Experience,
That she perceived herself
To feel
Like she was literally

In meaningfulness itself
With no need to search
For it
Nor to define the
Meaning of meaning
For the meaning
Was felt
From the inside out.

To this day,
She alludes to the experience
As
A path to meaningfulness.
To this day,
She has a way, a path
To experience
The meaningfulness
Of this day.

PEACE, HAPPINESS AND BLISS

Peace,
happiness,
bliss:
In that order.

She had been longing for
Peace in the center of her heart
And for peace in the open spaces
Of her mind and
Found it in her whole self
One day
When she learned
To literally release tenseness
From her entire body
Just by the simple act of
Letting go 'til tension
Dissipated to the four winds.

It was then that she experienced
How, indeed!
Mind and body work together
Acting as one,
For when she felt
Herself existing there,
In a body without tension,
She found herself simultaneously
(in there) resting ever so

Naturally in a
Calm
Comfortably cool
Collected state of mind.

Aha! That! She intuited
Is the stuff that constitutes
Peace, namely:
Quintessential calmness
The absence of irascibility
And a mind grounded
In an anchored
Sense of focus.

In order to preclude
The experience from eroding
She automatically went
To the memory bank of her
Mind and checked out —
As one does at a library —
A mental video tape
Which recorded one
Past experience of happiness.
In one flash of an awareness
She reviewed the contents
Of that happy experience.

While her inner self
Interwove those two states
Of being:
The peace she had gone to
In her inner space,
And the state of happiness
Evoked by her recollection
Of a fulfilling life event,
That selfsame inner self —
Like the unifying principle
Who it is —
Simultaneously felt
Itself immersed in what
She could only describe

As sheer bliss.
She felt life's celebration
Of her and her celebration.

PERFORMANCE:
ABILITY, MOTIVATION AND ENVIRONMENT

It was one of those mornings
When the sun didn't shine:
A day of gloom for the some,
One of reflection for others.

A recent reminder of the
Oft quoted:
"A life without reflection
Is one not worth living"
In turn reminded her
Of a great joy she was
Experiencing due to a
Wonderfully successful
Performance she had
Executed.

The reflection took her
To what had constituted
That performance.

There had been the ability
To perform
Which powers of the universe
Had provided by way of
Knowledge,
Techniques,

Skills,
Experience,
Tools to name but a few.

There had been motive
To perform
Which derives from
"Salt of the earth mantras"
And sutras and
Commonsensical reasons
For productivity and creativity,

And there had been provided
A physical and an emotional
Climate conducive to pushing
Within her the buttons
Which brought out the best
Within her to perform
At the level of excellence.

To this day
When she requests
Of the powers of the universe
Life in the form of successfulness
She asks for an equal dose
Of life in the form of
Understanding
What underlies successfulness*
And life in the form of fairness
In order for her
To give due credit where
Credit is due.

* Discovery of the principle that to perform successfully one
needs: ability, motivation and a positive environment.

ILLUMINATION, QUIETNESS AND STILLNESS

They simply found that:
In order to visit the frequency
Where being can be perceived
As its vibrant self
One needs to vibrate to the frequency
Enjoyed by
Unmitigated stillness and
Clear, cool quietness
And
To vibrate to these frequencies
Requires illumination —
Known as enlightenment by some.

It is the awareness of being
Which awakens one
To the presence of
The still and
The quiet.

The one awakening of
These two experiences of being
Turns on the light of
Illumination —
Known as enlightenment by some.

One does not bring on illumination.
It happens.

It occurs when one learns to be open
To what being can do.

The "being open"
Means
Staying present
To the quietness and
To the stillness of being itself.
The illumination
Will just be
And
When it is,
One is vibrating
At the frequency of being,
Perceiving being
As its vibrant self.

QUIETNESS, STILLNESS AND ILLUMINATION

He found it uplifting
To examine the wisdom
Flowing from the universe
Through historical teachers
Throughout the centuries
Of the world's cultures
And visited that examination
Precisely to access
Life
In the form of
Illumination.

Heights he ascended
Took him
To the throne
Of the presence
Of quietness
And to an audience
Of audiences
Of stillness
With stillness
And in stillness.

He experienced
The synergy of
The quiet and the still
Long enough
And frequently enough

And intensely enough
For the unfurling
Of enlightenment
Which those two aspects
Of being impart
In their process
Of illuminating the human
Experience.

In these profound journeys
He felt how
The unfurling enlightenment
Is coterminous with
The awakening of illumination.

THE SUN AND THE YELLOW DOT

He had read one day
What Picasso said one day
About
The yellow dot and the sun.

Some people, Picasso said,
Can take
A dot of yellow and
Make it a sun,
While others
Can take
A sun and
Make it a yellow dot.

This observation led this seeker
To asking the powers of the
Universe
To put him in the company
Of the ones
Who take dots of yellow
And create suns out of them.

He started wanting
The gift of creativity
And the more he requested it,
The more deeply he intuited
That there inherently
Exists a price to be paid

— not for the gift itself —
But for the creative force
To be birthed
Just as a mother
Pays the price
Of birth pangs
As she co-creates
With universal forces.

As creativity evolves,
He learns with increasing
Clarity,
That anyone can decide
To press for excellence
In the world of art;
One does not decide
What the world
Will deem artistically
Excellent.

A HUMAN OF ALL SEASONS

He simply wanted to be
A human of all seasons,
Accordingly, in his own way, at his own rate,
He asked
The authors of the seasons
— The powers universal —
To grant to him
The seeds one needs
To cultivate a perception
So broad and so deep
That one can view
Reality
From the varied perspectives
Seen by:
The teacher,
The ascetic,
The artist,
The socially minded,
The pragmatist,
And the leader
All at the same time.

These perspectives of the real,
He surmised,
Would enable him
To experience reality
As does the human of all seasons.

PRACTICALITY, COMMON SENSE AND SELF-CONFIDENCE

A student of life's
"What is and how it hangs together"
Sat in contemplation
Pondering:
How to extol
The value of the practical
(of all things)
And it came to him
Through thought association
That slang,
(of all things)
Is language used
By practical men and women
For its efficiency
And, as association of thought would have it,
He remembered
That Carl Sandberg
(of all people)
Had said of slang that
"It is language
Which spits in its hands
Rolls up its sleeves
And goes to work."

"Ah! So too", he figured,
Following that lead
We, too, could say that

Practicality is common sense
Slipping on gloves
And steel-toe-tipped boots
And trudging you with confidence
Through hell and high water.

He was trying to praise
The energy which comes in the form of practicality
And to do so in a practical way
And the idea
That being practical conveys.
Having confidence, too,
Had a sort of common sense
Appeal to him.

Practicality can so easily
Be characterized as
Vanilla mundane
And, thus, not be regarded
For the power
It generates.

Perhaps, he thought,
If we can continue
Propagating
How it ties in with common sense and with confidence,
Practicality can reach its apogee of appreciation
Among those who seek
To grow in their quest
For how else to be better
Than they were
The day before
In a world already
Chock full of
And saturated with
(of all things)
Mundane vanilla.

INNER VISION, SELF-HEALING AND BALANCE

He was quiet one night
and in that quietness
he dreamt a dream
and like it always is
this dreamer did not know
he was asleep:
the sleeper did not know
this was a dream
and in this dream
he met three spirits
who came into his presence
and they took him into theirs.

One spirit spoke
As the energy of inner vision,
One as the energy of self-healing
And the third
As the energy of the spirit
Of balance.

Each, he perceived
As a powerful spirit of
Powerful energy and a
Powerful energy of a
Powerful spirit.
This was no ordinary dream.

The spirits three revealed to him
That they move and reside
In the world of human intelligence
Through the frequency
Of consciousness and awareness
For from
Awareness and consciousness
They emerge, they revealed.

From the spirit of inner vision
He was learning
That there exists a
Way of knowing
Which transcends
The knowing of the waking state
And one which occurs
In the sacred space
Of the inner being
Whose presence is apprehended
Through awareness, (precisely),
Of the space within;
Learning that space has
the power to reveal.

In the dream state,
He resonated with
The spirit of self-healing
As a power which materializes
In the immune system
Residing in the bodies of
Intelligent and sentient beings
His own body included.

He was alert
To that unifying principle
Within himself which bestows
The power to regenerate physical energy
And to awaken more life
In a growing awareness
Of consciousness itself.

In this way, he was experiencing
That self-healing
Is a dual process
Affecting the body human
And the spirit
Of intelligent humans.

From the spirit of balance
He was coming in touch
With the reality of centeredness
— A state whereby
One instinctively avoids
"the too much" and
"the too little" and
Stays clear of being
" too here" or "too there,"
A state wherein
It is natural to intuitively
Observe
The Taoistic:
"Knowing when enough
Is enough" and
Setting "the string
Neither too tight nor too loose"
So that it can make
The sound of music.

The more meaning he was deriving
From these revelations
The more he was feeling
Like he was transmogrifying
From one dream-type to another.

He was feeling a shift
Within himself
Like when the mental picture
Goes from black and white
To full blown living color
And like the shift
Which people speak of
When they literally

Cascade from one paradigm
To another one altogether
While in the presence
Of the same reality.

In that shift he awakened
To the experience

That this was indeed
In a dream, but not of the surreal
World belonging to those
Who are unconscious
But in a dream like
Those in the altered state
Of heightened consciousness
In which the five physical senses
Are suspended.
And the conscious intelligence
— who one is —
is functioning at a higher
level of energy able to perceive
being existing at a higher
frequency than those
in the world of materiality.

He became one with
The three spirits
While he experienced
That, indeed and in fact,
They unfurled
From the intuitiveness
Of his own heightened
Awareness
And higher degree
Of consciousness in the quietness
Of the space
Of that one night.

TRANSFORMATION

She came to pass but did not stay
The one you loved and liked and kept so close.

He, just like her,
A fellow-wave (of yours and hers)
In life's ocean
Was and no longer is
In the form of W-A-V-E
But is in being-ness
Brought into consciousness
By the eternal awareness.

The two have gone
As you too will go
And be transformed
Like butterflies from caterpillar life
To life with wings
To fly to corners
Of outer boundaries
Of brand new space.

That's where she is
The one you loved
And he too, whom you thought special,
Is there too, where you will be,
All in trans-formation
And still in space, the place of the eternal space.

ABOUT "THIS TOO SHALL PASS"

Once upon a time
When he wasn't even aware
That inspiration comes from
The inner space
Of quietness and stillness,
He went to that inner space
And it occurred to him
That the wisdom of:
"This too shall pass"
Points out simply,
When life has been hard,
That you do not have to live
This day again,
Nor
Do you have to have
This breath again
When life is hard.

And when life is full:
"This too shall pass"
Poignantly reminds
So instructively,
That
You will not have this day
To live again
Nor
Will you have this breath

To breathe again.
Indeed!
"This breath is one breath less"
As: one has duly noted
About life, when it is full.*

*Hence the exhortation: "Do not squander"

TWO LITANIES

Once he had a secret wish
The way that secret wishers sometimes do
And that wish was for two litanies
To intersect and to merge
With each other
The way, we're told,
That galaxies can and sometimes do.

One of his litanies was (and is)
Of people whom he loves and has loved
Throughout phases
Of his earthly life.

That litany always starts
With his mother's name
And proceeds to list
People whose journeys
Have intersected and merged
With his and his with theirs
The way, we're told, that galaxies
Are known to do.

From such mergers has come
Many a unity
Like the one resulting
From the mutual interference
Of galactic bodies
Whose intersecting and merging

Become a celestial unity
Of magnificent strength and power.

(Sheer strength and power!)

The other litany envisioned
In his wish
Is of life forces
Which he perceives
As forces of life
Enhancing the quality of life
Of our mind, body and spirit
When those forms of life
Inform the life we experience.

The vision in his wish is for
All persons whose names he recites
In his first litany
To come to be able to receive
All the forms of life
Which he faithfully enumerates
In his second litany.

Both litanies are of his own making:
The first being people
Whom he values the most,
The second is of his most cherished values.

At will, he can add or subtract
From either litany and,
In point of fact,
He's added since first he began
And not a once has it felt needed
To subtract from either listing
So each has grown
As his awareness does.

The essence of his wish
Is that each person
He calls by name
And recalls by face

Receive unmitigated energy
From the powers governing life itself
And wishes that that energy
Comes in the forms he designates:
Life forces and
Forces of life
Which he envisions appearing
In the power inherent in:

Perspicacity
Insight
Awareness

Kindness
Generosity
Compassion

Health
Wealth
Humor

Peace
Happiness
Bliss

Successfulness
Understanding
Fairness

Love
Respect
Appreciation

Beauty
Harmony
Simplicity

Illumination
Creativity
Perceptiveness

Wisdom
Practicality
Acceptance

Faith
Strength
Protection

Inner–vision
Self-healing
Balance

Enthusiasm
Passion
Inspiration

Attention
Intension
Honor

And he envisions:

Stillness
Quietness
Oneness

It is the power inherent
In these realities
Which he wishes for
And the power therein inherent
Is the power of life itself
For from life its very self
That power flows and carries
The ability to manifest itself
In an infinite set of possibilities
Life having all of eternity
Within which
To convert the possible
Into the probable and
The probable into the certain
And the certain into "what-is."

In thus manner:
His wish – which he renews
Between every sunrise and every sunset –
Is to have those whom he loves
Participate more fully
In "All That Is" and
"All That Can Be" for them
As is manifested in
Those forms of life
Which he calls his second litany.

Picture this
His vision
In his wish:
One enormous group of
Selected persons
All forming like a galaxy
Of love-giving-sources
Intersecting and merging
With another galaxy
One of
Life giving forces
The two becoming one power
Of love and life
Brought into oneness
In his vision
In his secret wish
"which is no secret anymore."

ONE SILENT NIGHT

One silent night
In a pitch black place
He could visibly see
The cutting edge of the clarity
Of billions upon billions
Of sources of white heat
Up in the black black sky,
Where clusters of single stars
And free floating galaxies
And countless zodiacal
Configurations
Amidst galactic gas clouds
And endless vapor trails
All stood
— That silent night —
As if, in the stillness
Of eternity
And as if, transfixed
To simply breathe quietness.

He breathed in the stillness
And effortlessly
Inhaled the quiet,
Allowing the whole silent sky
To flow into his spirit
As if that celestial tableau
Could become

One silvery/golden thread
Of fire
With the power to stream-in
Like lasers do,
And once inside himself,
Resume its original shape
Inside the apprehending
Mind and heart and
Unifying principle within.

All that immensity and
The totality of that density
— He discovered, once more,
Just by looking up —
Can glow with equal intensity
In the light of his inner space
As it does
— this very instant —
In the darkness of outer space.

All of that immensity and
The totality of that density
Can glow with equal intensity
In the light of inner space
As it does
In the darkness of outer space.

Silent nights can do that to you.

QUALITIES OF COLORS

She had reached that level of consciousness
From which she could peer
Into further dimensions of reality beyond materiality
Where she could not so much see
But rather feel with an intuitiveness
The white of purity
The crimson of soothing feelings
The purple of passion
The royal blue of regal peace
The brown of earthen tones
The yellow in smiles
The pink of babies being babies
The rose of something eternal
The orange of musk
The grey of seriousness
The bleakness of outer space
The brilliance of inner space
The magenta of magic and the magic of magenta
The gold of values
The silver of the sincere
The bronze of the baranca de cobre – cliffs of copper
The tan of desert sand
The copper of sun rays
And besides the seven shades of green
Designing an oasis of hope
She could hear and taste the colors of the rainbow,
Including the searing red of burning love.

BLISS, JOY AND LOVE

He awoke to a level of consciousness
Where it felt like he was penetrating
Layers and layers of light and shadow
To where he could see flying beneath him
(For he was flying gracefully
At the speed at which photons travel)
The rapid passing of a territory
That went on and on
With size and dimension approximating
Nothingness and everything-ness simultaneously
And it extended for miles and miles in all
Of the directions of all points of the compass.

Finally, in this quasi-vision,
He came upon
One enormous remnant of a shell of a lonesome free-
standing
Structure
On this plain and strange landscape
Into which he kept hurtling past.
The structure reminded him of a a gargantuan gothic-like
Temple with multiple spires and towers
All reaching skyward above the clouds.

At the temple the hurtling stopped.
His vision took him slowly and quietly
To the inside space of these temple walls,
Which was host to vast spaciousness,

Solemn and majestic, serene and pacific.
Throughout the purity of that space
There crossed and crisscrossed
Streams and streams of rays of sunlight
Beaming through the rich colors
Of stately stained glass windows —

And all those rays were shades of gold — it seemed
No matter what color the glass
Which permitted their penetration
Into the vastness
Basking in those rays of sun power.
He next saw particles flowing.
Clearly he could see simple particles,
As if of dust — gold dust perhaps?
These particles barely moved
But none was still
And in their floating motion
They swayed up and down
And alternatively moved sideways
All movement was is if in reaction
To an invisible current
And the movement conveyed in consummate freedom
For the moveable to go in whatever direction
It chose to pursue.

In the flow of this total experience
he slipped into the awareness
Of a wide awake feeling
That in that giant cavernous expanse
Playing host to those floating particles
Of golden dust — perhaps, stardust of gold —
In those sun rays
One of those particles
Was his own spirit.

The unfurling metaphor was revealing to him
That he was observing himself
As he literally exists
In one dimension of the overall design
To which he belongs.

A design yet to be understood
But clearly one flowing in existence.

The deepening, the heightening and the broadening
Of awareness became more pronounced
As he realized
(In the quasi vision inside of a trance
Embedded in daydream)
That not only can he contemplate and experience
Realities such as Movement
Light
Golden
Dance
Current
Space
Color and
Invisible, He is these realities
In the flow of this one particular dimension
"Of All That Is And Is Becoming."
Just as he literally is
The breath he breaths
And these realities are him
And he knows not how
Nor does he need to know how
Since he already knows experientially
In What and Whom he participates
And in whom he swims and floats
And what and who swims and floats in him.

As the revelation continues (unfolding)
He finds himself in: A Bliss
                    : A Joy
                    : A Love (3 states of being)
And thereby in the awareness
the further awareness —
That he need not have power
To be powerful,
That he is full of power
As experienciable in the state of: Bliss
                                   : Joy and
                                   : Love

By simply living the whole experience
He apprehends at a visceral level (not a cerebral one)
That: he need not need to have to determine
what direction to take or seek in this dimension of life
That: he need not have to resist
the invisible variable currents
which invariably keep him in the design (of life)
and always keep him flowing
in the energy which is light (permeating all of life)
and keep him in proximity
to billions of trillions of
flecks or specks of golden stardust
all intelligent Aware-Energy-Fields, just as he is
and he need not need to know the name
of the terrain he's on (in life)
nor where it came from
nor where it goes
nor why it even resembles a temple housing space
and light rays.

The stillness in slow motion
The thundering quiet
The slow notion perfectly still
The silent thunder all simply
Transfix him in peacefulness, bliss, joy, love,
He becomes aware that he has found one way to understand
What he heard Mother Superior say many years ago in the
tale of *Dune* to Paul Muad'Dib when she said,
"The mystery of life is not a problem to be solved,
but a reality to experience."

Made in the USA
San Bernardino, CA
24 January 2020